DECADE DANCE

DECADE
DANCE

poems by
Michael Lassell

Boston : Alyson Publications, Inc.

This is a trade paperback original from
Alyson Publications, Inc., 40 Plympton St., Boston, Mass. 02118.
Distributed in Great Britain by GMP Publishers.

First edition, first printing: September 1990

Library of Congress card catalog number
90-43181

ISBN 1-55583-179-6

In memory of
Kenneth G. Moore and J. Clark Henley,
whose deaths cast such
long shadows.

CONTENTS

"'Tis certain there's not a boy left alive,
and the cowardly rascals that ran from the battle
ha' done this slaughter."

—William Shakespeare
Henry V, Act IV, Scene 7

ACKNOWLEDGMENTS

Grateful acknowledgment is made to the editors of the following publications, in which many of the poems in *Decade Dance*, some of them in slightly different forms, first appeared: *Amelia, Bay Windows, Central Park, City Lights Review, The Colgate Portfolio, Hanging Loose, The James White Review, Kansas Quarterly, Poetry/LA,* and *ZYZZYVA*. In particular, I would like to thank Robert Hershon and Frederick A. Raborg, Jr., for their generosity, and for their early and ongoing support.

"How to watch your brother die" was first published in *Poems for Lost and Un-Lost Boys* (Amelia, 1985), my previous volume of poetry. It was later included in two anthologies in which I am proud to have my writing appear: *Gay and Lesbian Poetry in Our Time* (St. Martin's, 1988), edited by Carl Morse and Joan Larkin, two excellent poets who have become friends; and *Poets for Life: 76 Poets Respond to AIDS* (Crown, 1989), edited by the poet Michael Klein, who has been unceasing in his advocacy. The "Times Square Poems" also appeared in *Gay and Lesbian Poetry in Our Time*.

On a purely personal level, I want to express my thanks to Eric Latzky, Michael Nava, and James Carroll Pickett, three men who became my brothers in the time of my deepest despair; to three Bills—Hill, Pryor, and Meredith—in whose lives I see the value of my own; to Richard LaBonté, for his evangelism on my behalf; to Paul Monette, who put the rage in courage, and who leads by his example; to Barry Sandler, the best movie date in L.A.; to the tribe of gay and lesbian poets who have welcomed me with loving arms, including, in no particular order: Yves Lubin, Christopher Hewitt, Mark Ameen, Essex Hemphill, Dennis Cooper, Jewelle Gomez, Alfred Corn, Marilyn Hacker, Rudy Kikel, Minnie Bruce Pratt, David Trinidad, Ron Schreiber, Eloise Klein Healy, Eileen Myles, and, of course, Gavin Dillard, whose friendship goes back to CalArt days, and who was, without question, the most beautiful boy I have ever seen.

I would also like to thank, for a variety of good, but private, reasons: Roy Cameron, Gerry Ayres, Don Bachardy, Andrew J. Mellen, Robert Drake, Sharon McDonald, Dan Hart, Joie Davidow, Ingrid Sischy, A Different Light bookstores, Tina Summerlin and the Mapplethorpe Studio, The Kitchen, Ira Silverberg, Amy Scholder, George Stambolian, John Preston, Terry Wolverton, Michael Denneny, Sasha Alyson, and Linda Ekblad, my "sister," who has been there from the beginning and who has always been an inspiration. My thanks, too, to Danny, Julio, Kevin, and other past and present members of the fraternity; forgive me if you don't recognize yourselves, or if you do.

There is one more debt to pay, and that is a debt of love, to Ben Mah, my partner of ten years. Although we are no longer together, he was, and is, the best part of my heart, my only comfort in the midst of the nightmare.

—Michael Lassell
New York City
July, 1990

I.
Dancing Days

Dancing days

For Yves Lubin,
poet and dancer

We were dancing.
We were always dancing
in the dancing days.

We danced without shirts,
the buttons of our jeans·
open as our nipples.

And we were dancing,
and the music was loud,
and our bodies were always

smiling panther muscle,
dawn-to-dawn endurance;
we were always wet.

There was no need for Paris;
we were sated patriots of
bacchanalian spring,

tossing conquests
over proud heads from
one to another like

medicine balls
to pump our
bulging sinew up.

Our hair was bright and long,
our hopes high and limitless.
We were always hot and innocent

in the dervish disco lights,
kissing long and restive nights
of hard flesh and tongues.

Until the needle of
spoiled tattoos
began to infect us:

nocturnal bubbles burst,
day skin erupted with
unknown consequence.

Blood turned to
sand in our veins,
our hair began to dry,

to fall like autumn leaves
in chemotherapy winds.
We were shocked.

We put on suits and underwear.
The music stopped.
We sat on the sidelines, sapped.

We pined for France,
for friends and the old familiar;
each tentative embrace became a pietà.

We dropped our eyes
and were our fathers
a generation too soon.

In the dancing days we did not
march in funerals
bearing lovers on low shoulders,

did not weep or shout or
pass out leaflets in public—
we were only dancing ... *dancing!*

We were naked,
hairless, smooth.
We were yes and now:

our weekly broken hearts
found solace in the next dance,
the promise of a stranger

poised on the darkened outskirts
waiting to wrap us
in rhythmic limbs.

And we danced without future,
and we danced without past
in the long gone dead and deadly

dancing days
before the dirge began
and death was born.

II.
Before the Deluge

Keenings: After Rilke

(lamentations for baritone and chorus)

For Eric Torgersen

1.
Ground rules at an empty bar
on a rainy afternoon

"I'm about as interested in her,"
he said,
"as I am in the laws governing
nuclear thermodynamics."
He took a drag on his cigarette and
looked for a moment like someone who
might in fact have been obsessed
with science in a previous decade
(a long-nosed youth or silent child
with a red tin box of chemicals).
"People addicted to conformity,"
he continued,
"are bloodless, tone deaf."

I touched the ash of his cigarette,
still warm in the black
eyeglass-plastic ashtray,
and smiled at the recitation.
He was learning.

I took the cigarette from between
two fingers of his left hand,
put it in my mouth, and
smoked it for a while.
He was put out, but
pretended to enjoy
the sharing.

The fat bartender slapped a fly
from his old tattoo with the bar rag,
turned the baseball game off the radio,
and sat crying while a boys choir sang
a Renaissance *Stabat Mater.*

"Why are you grinning?"
you asked
as my smile broadened.
"I don't know," I said,
a tune beginning to
turn in my mind;
"I was just thinking that
life is waged in the
pronouns voyeurs use
to explain themselves to God."

"Christ," you said,
 licking the beer from your upper lip and
trying to get the waiter's attention,
"you are too much."

2.
Jesse and the beggar

Jesse sits in the hot light
of the plastic kitchenette
barechested over loose jeans.
The Gothic towers of the college
rise behind him
through an open window.

The muscles of my jaw
work out his curves,
my eye takes him in
from the sofa by the door
(as full of contours as
his shoulder draped across a chair).

"No," he says,
looking over the faded yellow tabletop,
"I can't."
"Why?" I press.

Jesse sits in the hot light,
his face pulled together in the
center like a fist,
an angry fist had grabbed it
and milked the liquid
from the life it
found there.

I feel the hair on my neck crawl
as if he were ten feet closer
with his mouth
empty of objections and
full of me
(the unfed desires of his childhood
focused on a white-hard nipple).

Truck tires bounce the building.
He lets the tremor subside,
looks up, hurt,
pensive:
"No," he says,
"I've tried. It doesn't work."

I contrive a tear for the silence.

He drops his eyes like bullets,
turns them back again:
"No," he says,
"I really can't."

There's
a finality this time
in the easy way he
swallows his drink and
stands to leave, but:

Truck tires shake the building
and the quaking does not stop;
the Gothic towers of the university
topple under scrutiny.
Before your eyes
the building is rent asunder
like the veil of the tabernacle,
and Jesse
falls to the floor
crushed in the temblor of
my insatiable longing.

3.
Blind in the shadow of a mountain

"You're wrong," Ruth said,
lifting her soft black hand
from his hard white forearm.
"Nobody likes him. We
only put up with him
because of you."

The words hit his ear like
stone on stone, sound
but no sense;
he did not see
the truth in the words.
How could he? He was always blind,
blind with love,
blind with rage,
eternally grateful for
your pulling me out of the abyss
and holding me inside you
night after night,
grateful for civil meals taken
with disapproving mothers,
grateful that you relented
after the third apology
every time.

Of course he could not see it,
until later, when placing a
softer hand on the brown arm
of a shorter stranger,
he tried to determine sex
by odor alone and decided
he did not care to know
anything more
about music.

4.
A toast to the prodigal
as he sets off to the whores

The family sat in a circle of lawnchairs
like a ring of toadstools,
eating hot dogs and singing songs,
retelling their stories to others who
could not care less:
a drunken accident, the handmade dress
she was ashamed to wear,
just as she was ashamed
of her father's accent.
An uncle with instant opinions on anything
made my head swim,
full as it was of televised tall ships
sailing under the
Narrows Bridge I
drove across once to my own
Princeton charmer,
the one who loved
lemon chicken
and quoting
Proust in bed *en français*
and the idea of me.

As the sun set on Independence Day,
I switched from gin to

cool old friendly Scotch on
rocks of purified ice
water, watched her wonder
how much I would drink
that night and
what it would do to
the shape or
brevity of a smile.

"Have a wonderful time in California,"
the madwoman said,
pressing a folded ten-dollar bill
into his hand like the philosopher's stone.
"Have a drink on me."

A bottle later I was
completely in its power and felt
nada, as the Puerto Ricans say.
Times Square was a house of a
different nut after the suburbs and
I wandered across 42nd Street past
seventeen hundred and seventy-six
separate offers of licit or
illicit drugs
and found you
in a darkened booth
at the back of a bookstore
behind a half-closed door.

Your pants were so
full of you
as you dropped quarters
into the movie slot,
I felt unworthy—but
the alcohol was game,
and I was
on my knees
feeling like a fool and
wanting another drink
before it was even
over:
you pushing me away,
hitting me on the cheek with
your knee,
zipping your fly
without a word,
running from my
pigsty forever
before I even knew
your name.

Your name might have been something to
pin it on,
at least once.

5.
Unaccompanied suicide in bed at home

The death of a man I hardly knew
was not easier to accept
just because the man was me,
although it was, perhaps,
less surprising than it might have been.

"He put a rifle barrel
into his mouth," she said,
"and pulled the trigger
with his toe.
Patrick found him."
There was a note
explaining it all
in simple
unemotional terms:
"After years in a sewer
I have come to see life at its best.
I find it
lacking something
I require."
There was blood everywhere,
blood, shock, and hunger.

Dennis was a fool
to make such a
mess of it. I'd
want my own death to be
a capella, the only sound
in a lay cathedral.

Others wept through the memorial
without taking it as a cue
to follow suit
one way or another.
It's not
that I am without hope;
all my hopes realized, I'd
still feel cheated,
angry,
condemned.
The stars through the pine trees
glint like bathroom light
on the steel edge of a razor.
Make no mistake,
I am fully capable of
passing an hour, chilled to the bone,
miming the last
incisive moment,
an imagination full
of the deaf blade
sliding lateral down a vein.

In the end
I chose pills
and watched you
drop off.
Your hands on the bed closed
like dead spiders.
Then it was over,
nothing unexpected
having occurred,
except for the particularly
vivid red of the vomit
on my chin.

6.
The grief of an unmarried widow
in a distant place

After he died
and the court had pronounced me a stranger—
legally speaking—
I inherited, that is,
came into, that is,
was bequeathed for my years:
his half of the charges
on my credit cards.
I blew my nose,
delivered an unimpassioned speech
in the vilest terms I could conjure
to a judge who grew blue in the face,
and went home
and died myself
one more time.
His cousins were going through our clothes
while County marshals
cracked bored jokes
about him
and me, but
I had no feelings, only
the impatience a stranger might experience
at a funeral procession
crossing a busy intersection at noon.

I dressed in bright colors,
blood red and hate yellow,
withdrew my life savings from the local bank
where they knew
us
by name, and
headed to the street where
the boy hustlers worked to old age
or young death. I
fucked them one by one for
fifty bucks a throw
until the money was gone and
I had forgotten him
to become one of you.

7.
Idiotics in the State Preservatory

I'm only an idiot because I choose to be.
I could just as well become a saint, but
who could spend eternity
listening to the half-assed whining prayers of
whatever pack of pathetic losers
I might be appointed patron of?
I'd rather be an idiot.
It's cheap and it's easy.

Got a cigarette?

Just the other day
Christ Almighty was offering me
anything I wanted—Christ
is a lousy pederast in Ward B.
We make rugs together
from the bloody stockings of
Italian virgins.

Sure, sure, I know.

If you could get me out of here, I'd
sing you a tale
would stand your hair on end,

would topple the topless towers of
whatchmacallit... Sure I
screwed the cunt, she had it coming.

Fuckin' ingrate, that's what he is.

At first I just sat there kind of glad
nothing else could happen and sort of
rolled into a ball. They shocked me out of it,
but before that I wanted to be somebody.
First I wanted to be somebody and then I
wanted to be somebody else, yes,
that was it: somebody, *anybody*
else.

Even as a kid I knew buttercups were
more cow than chaos.

If you could get me out of here, I'd
make my bed every morning and
pull weeds. I'd miss my friends, though,
the bald bitch who
shits quarters, the
nurse who
sucks my dick when
no one's looking and hits me with a club
when they are. I

guess I learned my lesson now,
can swallow my pride, which
goeth before, goeth before...

I fell on the ice.
I wanted to be somebody else.
I loved the asshole.
Then you sent me here,
patron saint of children
too cowardly to
put up a fight.

Bishop says there's worms in us all,
ain't that right, Jack?
There's worms in the cookies anyway,
that's what Jane said.

8.
Orphans and asylums

Naomi got to be an orphan
after her father killed himself,
her mother having died already, and
Naomi cried nonstop for
thirteen years in the old State Home.
Then she had a malformed son
and choked to bloody death
trying to swallow the
umbilical cord, leaving another
unfathered thing behind her in the world.

(Of all my fears, her leaving was the worst.
By the time I knew she would never go, my
fantasies were all of my own stillbirth.)

Why did you hate me that
May Sunday thirty years ago?
I was a child,
could see it in your eye.
You claimed to be my mother but
did not speak to me
all day. Natural mothers
don't act that way. That's why
I stayed home from school and
searched your papers for the

certificate and told Elizabeth
I was adopted.

You haven't understood a thing about me since
I learned not to speak.

9.
Dwarves *en la calle de los sueños*

"It's only that my
legs are short," he said
standing on a box
before his easel,
staring at the model with
his paintbrush poised,
"and my moral sense
a bit truncated,
perhaps.
That's all."

"I don't mind about that," she said
hiking her skirt
a bit higher on the thigh,
"I'm used to small men.
Still, it must be odd
to be so small."

"I once knew a whore," he said,
"who pronounced me
the perfect height to
suck cock or eat pussy
without having to
bend over or lie down."
He wondered where to put the paint

now that he'd gathered it onto his brush.
"And then," he continued,
"expectations are so low
you get enough room to
live a life in."

"Christ," she said,
"I could use some of that.
Still, it must be odd
not to be normal."

"Angelica," he sighed,
the mood spoiled by his having
touched the brush to the canvas,
"I'm just an overweight
middle-aged man who walks around
with an angry forehead on
as often as not.
I see misery on the faces
of Spaniards at bus stops or
a woman in a yellow bathrobe
raking leaves in a rainy street,
and I set it down. That's all."

But the explanation did not
satisfy her, so she went home,
took off all her clothes,
and knelt in front of a mirror

trying to imagine
what a head that size must feel like
or having a hand too small
to hold a breast
as perfect as her own
and about the lovers of castrati
descanting a madrigal
for a virgin queen.

10.
Metropolitan leprosy

The first time someone shouted the obscenity
through a car window
it was just my skin was bad.
I wasn't beaten for it until later,
when the warts
began to grow warts and
the big ones began to bleed.
The first time I woke in a doorway
I looked down at a gray cat was
batting a fingernail around and a
bit of skin that
had come loose in the night.
After I lost the first joint of three fingers
and the second of another, they
set me on fire in Echo Park, but
I was too quick for them and
jumped into the lake. I
don't want to die by fire.

I was never beautiful, but
there was a time
I didn't frighten animals.
Insects still light on me, even butterflies,
dogs still lift their legs.
Can you imagine, can you remember

the time it would have spoiled my day
just to find a scratch on a favorite record,
a Schumann mass, for example,
how you carried on when I trimmed
the parakeet's claws and left
blood on the newspaper?

Now I am exiled in cities.
I forgive you, why not?—I'm not God.
The winos ate the swans in the park,
but the birds were already dead.
The foreign boys killed them
instead of me.
I still love you;
you condescend to slap my face
by your long-distance hatred and
cold, close-quartered indifference.
I know,
you need to save your own skin.

I understand, and
it's enough. God knows.
It's enough.
Why should you die too?

III.
Street Meat

Melissa Marie

Melissa Marie is a Cuban drag queen who thinks of herself as a Spanish-American princess. She got beat up on Saturday night in the parking lot behind the Beef Bowl by two white boys looking for real pussy and no surprises.

Melissa Marie glides into The Plaza on silver heels like skates on ice. She is not indignant. She's shaded the eye bruise with a blue liner lifted from Thrifty's to match her sequined gown.

Melissa Marie takes a drag on Nando's Kool and blows smoke through long lashes. "Shit, man, Nando," she says, "after the pigs in Havana and the food in Castro's jail, a girl can take any goddamned thing, *verdad?*"

Nando's got a scorpion's temper but no green card, so Melissa Marie talks him down. "Fuck, man, it ain't shit. Just shows how good I am. Serves me right for gettin' took off guard."

But Marie's got a memory as long and hard as her lacquered nails, and she's packing a shiv in her jet reticule. And two white boys last seen coming out of Gino's got Death written all over their narrow yellow backs.

Bon voyage

KimBurly the Korean she-man took a piss on a post behind the Buick dealership, shook out her dick and pulled up his pantyhose. Kim-Burly had the biggest balls any woman ever had and silicone tits to match. You could see them free in a dozen porn rags at any emporium of erotica worth its lube license. KimBurly stood on the B-vard bragging at her friends how she met this rich dude with a Rolls was going to take her off the street and make her Madame Thing. Trouble was the rich dude wanted Kim's thing cut off, and that was out of the question, no way. Meanwhile, Daddy Big Bucks liked sucking Kim off and moaning "Nice Pussy," so Kim sometimes had a hard time keeping a straight face. Anyway, Easy Street was just around the corner and

"There he is!" she screamed, as a seasoned Pontiac slid to a halt under blue neon and scrutiny. "That ain't no Rolls," spat TJ — and the ugly driver didn't look too high-heeled either. Loyal to ideals, Kim shot a withering glance at the offending fact fanatic and drew herself up to retort: "Of course it's a Rolls, you stupid bitch. What else kind of car would Prince Charming own?" And KimBurly the Korean she-man got into that badly polished pig, and she ain't been heard from since.

Pool

Oh Frank, you shrewd dude, swimming nude in an aqua-blue pool under the loose gaze of a dozen would-be moguls. They watch you slice the water, rippling the surface of your hairless thighs, and the odor of chlorine inches into flared nostrils. Your backstroke smile goes to the heart and cuts studs to geldings. They make deals over you, the way the chilled flesh of your chest quivers when you step into a cool breeze in afternoon (and the life in your lap as it leaps to attention just knowing they covet you).

Where did you learn this water ballet, Iowa farmboy? Was it practiced with your floating in a wheat-soft womb to blossom in the lush greed of a southern landscape?

Knowing you has taught me my age.

Punk love

Hard as nails and wrapped in leather, the punk's white butt was smooth as snails when I stripped the street off him and slipped into his head through his asshole. His collar and cuffs were studded with metal, his torso with constellations of moles. He'd cinched up his dick in a miniature bridle and shot silver arrows through pity-filled nipples that blushed to the touching.

Licking him senseless was an act of mercy.

Kevin

The curled black hairs
of the Puerto Rican callboy
lay on the hotel pillow
like commas in a series of
empty gestures.

Kiss me, he said
just before he came
and he kissed me again
before going.
In between:
the wide expanse of
shoulds and sheets,
his purple lips/sweet skin/
perfect teeth
all over me,
stories of his seven friends José,
the warmth of a body at
long long last,

an idle hour
washed clean by
soap/shampoo/
a hundred-dollar bill
and the click clack
of the double lock
behind him.

You couldn't even hear
a footfall on the plush
corridor carpet;
you couldn't hear the lie
in his flattery, either,
or the time allotted
in his leisure.

Claudio

Claudio has a new tattoo,
a cobra twisting on his
fisting forearm,
echoing
as he dances
the smaller snake that's
flicking tongue forks over
loose Jockeys.

It's Thursday and
he's stripping slow,
sooo bored
he can barely keep his prick stiff.

There are tattoos on his
lost youth too,
those inky lines that
Dorian his face all
gray New York.
Once he was sweet
Canadian bacon
flipping tricks
till he got his feet
on the ground.

Now they're in the air
as often as not; his
attitude's as old as
juggling.

One of the others says it's
coke that's
etched a map on
Claudio's hollowing eye.
His thighs survive,
hard and smooth through his
mute soft shoe,
limp in the knees and
no longer shy.

After his set he's
on the prowl for man-dollars,
50 bucks a private show.
He used to make you come
to him and wasn't all that keen
to be touched by strangers.
He's taken down the
Hands Off sign and
lays his greed intentions
on your cool indifference like
a faded anchor
riding the bread-soft shoulder
of an ancient salt

rolling up his tattered sleeves
for day work.

You're eager but
wait for dancer number two,
a Florida kid who knows what
flesh is all about
and isn't ashamed to let you know
he likes it.

Casey/jones

Casey gives nickel blow jobs
in the quarter peeps on Eighth off 42nd
to support his habits:
heroin, humiliation, and men.

Nights he seduces with eyes like
Dietrich's on the *Shanghai Express*,
muffler wrapped around his face
like a sultan's numero uno.

He's just in from Philly,
or so he says. Like as not
he'll be dead before New Year's:
If the drugs don't kill him
or the plague,
the druggists will
or John Q. Homo-erectus
with a steel-edged hard-on.

"You want me to use a rubber?"
I ask,
safe in the shark's tank,
but his mouth's already full.
His eyes say it's a new question and
way too real, man, way too real.
He keeps those mandibles working
without a word.

He knows
how to serve
and how
to get what he wants
and how
to make you think in passing
there's no one else on earth but you, babe,
no one but you.

His dick is small and soft,
his belly smooth and white like
Garbo in *Camille:*
flawless porcelain and doomed.

Who's using who?
Ask me later. He needs more
than me, and I need nothing at all
except him: Casey and his aching jones.

"I'm going to come," I say,
my body dripping sweat,
winter heat pounding in my head without
cracking into thought.
It's over
in no time.
In no time,
I'll want him again.

I hand him a ten for

good behavior.
He knows where to look a gift horse
and how
to look grateful
instead of ready to be sick.
He dresses with practiced aplomb.
His chaste kiss is
wet and
cold with semen.

"Usually I'm kind of wary about goin' anywheres,"
he says,
"but now I know you, okay?"
he says,
like we just signed a seven-year contract
with options,
his eyes like Marilyn's
when she goes back to drinking alone in
Some Like It Hot.

Days Casey watches at the
Show Palace threshold of
porn and panting,
vamping tricks from the streets like a pro-
fessional fisher of men.
Days he wears a conning rap
strung-out like pearls:
"There's some spiritual shit, some spiritual shit
goin' down in the basement,"

he says,

"in the basement of the hotel,
some satanic shit,
somethin' 'bout a dead baby
in the basement of the hotel,"

he says,

"and some woman jumped off the
twentieth floor,
I don't know, I seen her."

He asks me for quarters and
another waltz in his
two-by-two confessional booth, but he's
crazy now with eyes like
Swanson's in *Sunset Boulevard*,
ready for his closeup,
Mr. DeMillionaire,
and the poppy rot has
cut black spots into his teeth,
his lips are split and scarred,
and I was a fool
to touch him,
and he was a fool
to touch back,
and there we stand
on Eighth off 42nd,

two cool fools with a jones on
out to score some serum truth
to get us through another day of
bloodless ritual.

Times Square Poems

1.
Gino

This morning I clipped my nails,
in case I ran into Gino again.
Gino's a stripper at the
Gaiety Burlesk on 46th off
Broadway, the last of six dancers
five times daily and
well worth the wait.

There's only one way to
run into Gino
and it isn't by chance:
pay your six bucks at the door—
five if you've got a coupon from
The Village Voice—then
poke around in the dark with
the other fat fruits until
the lights come up and
decorum goes down like
the *Titanic.*

Last night,
in the small room
behind the stage,

he brought me off for
25 bucks as
one finger of my
right hand
wormed into
his asshole.

I carried the smell of him
home with me—
talc, sweat, and fear. I mean,
hygiene has its place, but
I let him linger. I
wasn't about to
wash him off as if
he'd never been there.
I owed him more than
the canned scent
housewives use to
freshen up
their porcelain.

2.
The going rate

The going rate is
40 bucks but
some of them will
do it for less weekdays.
Alberto did it for
30 because I was
"nice."

Tony said he'd go with me
for 20 but
Tony's got a dollar sign
cut into the hair at the
back of his head, and
Tony is not
Alberto, though
it was sweet of him
to offer.

In the back room
Alberto slips off his
clothes, then
mine. There is no
kissing, of course,
nothing that might
leave a mark on his

pride. Alberto's straight,
you see, or so he says.
Still, he's more direct
than most people you'll encounter
on a Thursday.

I come fast and apologize:
my semen gets
on his shoe.
"Part of the work," he says
with an accented grin and
wipes it off, then me.

If you want to
get off with Alberto
bring cash
and believe when he says
"I like you" that he's
never said it before
and won't again
before sunrise.

3.
Stud

His name is Jason; he's
"Italian" and "twenty."
Actually, Jason is the name of
whoever is dancing third
because that's what
the sign says out front
(these boys do have
a following).
He starts his second dance with
a hard-on that
softens in the
shuffle for
attention, but
it's never lost
for long.

Jason has a
lot of admirers.
Also a wife and child in
Puerto Rico.
Between shows—after a
"private performance" that
leaves him sapped
and sweaty as
a cane cutter—
he tries to call

San Juan on
the pay phone to see if
they came through
the hurricane
unscathed.

Of course, the phones
are out, lines
down, signals
dead.

He has the eyes of a Virgin and
pecs like the gifts of the Magi:
gold for wealth because he is
king of the roost;
frankincense because he is
the high priest of the
low in heart;
myrrh for cunning
because it heals my soul
just to look at him
and to know that
as long as there's money
there's a hairy chest
for my hand
somewhere in the world—
and I'll never go hungry
again.

4.
How to find love in an instant

Sit as close to the stage as possible.
Look like you're one of the kind who's buying and
like you've got the wherewithal.
Look into his eyes.
Look into his lap.
Covet him as loud as you can without speaking.
Do not touch. Just worship silently.

Applaud; show
appreciation. At the end of the set
let him approach you in the lounge where
Boys Meet Boys. He will put
one hand on your left tit and one on the
tight bundle of your jeans and
offer a private session for 40 bucks.
If you've got it, give it.
Don't dicker.

After you're both naked, he'll
rub his oiled body against yours.
You will be hard and hot and
grateful. He will be soft and bored
but attentive.

You will walk out into the night and no longer be
afraid of 42nd Street.
Now you are a part of it
and the locals can tell.
You will smile to have been accepted
and descend the subway stairs
knowing yourself better than ever
and better than ever
thinking yourself just fine.

For John,
since I cannot be his lover

1.
What hit you

It was the eyes. It usually is. There's no surprise in that. If I could love the eyes without taking on the bodies attached, I'd be a happy man. But eyes are caught in a tangle of veins, arteries, optic nerves that clutch a brain where impossible dreams grow like milkweed, and dreams wilt into disappointments before you even know what hit you.

2.
In the shadows

I looked into his eyes and there
was need. There was pain, too.
You could see it between the tight
pale skin and high white bones of
his face. I could see unkept prom-
ises in the space between his thin
brows and across the bridge of his
sharp, straight nose. His eyelids
were luxury enough to betray a
pampered childhood, recently
abandoned, or indulgent school-
ing abroad. He was standing in the
street, looking like he belonged
there, leaning one foot up on the
outside wall of a new wave club
all the music rags were saying was
happening like crazy. I was in the
market for meat, but when I first
laid eyes on him, I said "Oh" out
loud. A stronger desire than I'd felt
in years dropped from my throat
into my lap, an elevator freed from
its cable.

3.
John, in the guise of David

From what I could see, and I couldn't
see much, the chest was hairless. I
wanted more; I pulled the shirt apart.
The nipples were small and flat like
copper nickels. He had a tattoo over
his heart. It was simple, but well
wrought: a cross. There was a J on
each side of it. "They call you JJ?"
I asked. "John," he said and looked
out from under his blue eyelids. The
pink light from the cool neon sign
slid along the grease he had used to
hold his curly hair in place. He smelled
sweet, like the memory of ham and
cloves. He had a mole on his upper
lip where the sneer should have been.
It was adequate shot for his sling.

4.
First date

He lived on a dead street in the hot
flats of Hollywood, under the sign
and a layer of night smog and greed.
Even in the dark you could see the
mindless pink of the stucco walls. It
was the kind of profligate place took
its cue from a sleazy motel movie of
the nineteen-fifties: turquoise doors
with knobs set in pitted brass star-
bursts, locks you could pick with a
credit card, no sweat.

The wall by his bed was covered with
crosses. There must have been fifty of
them or more, the largest about a
yard long from the bowed and
bloody head of Jesus C. to his feet, a
miracle of muscle and bone. Most
were antique, many ornate. Some
had red votive candles in front of
them on sconces nailed to the wall.
He lit the candles and lifted a small
silver cross from around his Saint
Sebastian's plaster neck and hung it
around my own. He kissed me once

on each cheek, a kindly old bishopric fruit at an ordination. Then he kissed me again, not quite so much a cleric. My wet lips moved after him, but he put one pointed finger to my chest and said, "You want a drink?" then moved off toward the kitchen.

5.
Sex

I kept trying to focus on the craggy bulge of his trachea in that tight neck of his. I kept thinking how easy it would be to slit it with a straight razor. I kept thinking that the purpose of flesh is to disguise physical function, the purpose of art to deconstruct the camouflage, the purpose of sex to slash the canvas. My head was rolling from side to side on the pillow like a sleeping man's on an ocean voyage. I was pumping up into him wondering how much longer I could keep going. Suddenly he looked down into my eyes, opened his mouth in surprise, dropped his head behind him and sprayed me with his semen, like a randy cat or the gods of the sea. I found myself staring into his eyes while tears of unspecified origin slid down his sweaty face onto the gray hairs of my beard. I felt old. His hips in my hands felt like the creation of longing in a careless moment.

IV.
Rendezvous with Death

The Ides of August

In my dream
there are two men:
one is wasted, thin;
one is young with waist-length hair.

In my dream
there is skin;
shame is blinded by
light off laughter.

August is not for loving.

At the cemetery
I stare at the replica David
(restored after the
earthquake took him).
Michelangelo pinched the boy
from off the streets and made him
immortal. But what was his name?
And how did he feel, warm
in the stonecutter's arm?

Zachary is three and
counts David's toes,
each as big as a toddler's hand,
tries to lift the giant from his

pedestal: his father
protects him from failure.

Kenny has taken his AIDS to Lake Tahoe,
Clark keeps his cool under San Francisco skies.
Zachary lost a sister this week, his mother says.
She was stillborn and buried on Wednesday
near "a nice path" in the Court of Freedom.

In the morning
names claim the flesh of my dream men:
stroke-surviving, epileptic Peter and
Midwestern Michael from '72 (let me remember).

August is not for loving.

Driving home I catch
the eyes of a
shirtless boy
selling himself on the
boulevard.
His chest is sculpted.
Hair cascades around his
cold shoulders.

And I want to make love to
Peter and Michael from out of the past;
Kenny and Clark, men without future;

skin-perfect David who danced away;
and three-year-old Zachary when he comes of age;
and the nameless boy who took off his shirt to
move his wares and found a place in me
where he lingers long after
the curtain comes down on his
rearview mirror stage.

August is not for loving.
Neither are dreams.

Surviving

Bill LaV tells me
Steven R has died,
wasted from a strapping Nordic youth
to witless nothing:

How are you, Steve?
  How am I, Mom?
    You're fine, honey.
I'm fine, honey.

Eating burgers with
Michael N, chatting of
positive and negative,
incest survival floats between us,
his evil uncle lurking in the pauses
like an obsequious waiter.
And I am wondering if Tony is
ever going to sleep with me,
or whether I'll ever get a job
that doesn't steal more than it pays,
and why it matters if I die
of a heart attack anyway.

Do you have a fever, Steve?
  Do I have a fever, Mom?
    No, honey, you don't.
No, honey, I don't.

The police chopper,
beloved of insomniacs,
circles the block for an hour
shining a searchlight into
darkened windows, but
it's only an urban annoyance,
not the beacon that I seek,
and the fugitive slouching in the alley
is only a felon at large,
not a reason to go on.

Are you breathing, Steve?
  Am I breathing, Mom?
    No, honey, you're not.
  No, honey, I'm not.

Pietà

A man who is ill
visits his mother
in her nursing home.

You don't look well, she says.
Neither do you, he says.

My friends are all dying, she says.
My friends are dying, too.

I'm afraid that when I die
there will be no one left to
say prayers at my grave, she says.
It's my fear, too, he replies.

And they sit and weep,
each dropping tears onto
the hands of the other,
waiting for the after
that follows hard
the heels of time.

How to prepare
for the death of a friend

For Clark and for Sharon

Start early.
Begin to withdraw when he tells you
T-shirt simple
he hasn't yet broken
his glory-hole habit.

Be cool when the first symptoms crop up
in conversation over tea and croissant brunches.
You'll be seeing less and less of him
in the months to come.
After all, you have your work
and he has his: cradling others
into death. Roads diverge.

By the time the diagnosis blossoms
you'll already be forgetting to
answer his phone calls or
ask about T-cells.

Denial is a messy business, but it beats
mourning.

You'll help him move back North,
of course, what are friends for?
You'll pack his billion books and
tape shut the file boxes with their
fake wood grain—
stackable,
disposable.
Joke all day; do not say *death*.

After all, he isn't family.
Why *shouldn't* they take care of him?
They brought him into the world, didn't they?
They fucked him up.
Let *them* change his diapers when the time comes.
Maybe they'll do a better job
this time.

What are you talking about?

You didn't share bathtubs as boys or
climb into bunk beds as children,
but you slept and showered together
as men.
And if you never filled the same womb,
you shared at least a matricidal rage at
women who prefer decorum
to sons.

He'll call/
you'll call,
will write/will write,
will even visit—both ways—
sit bedside,
stare into blue eyes,
kiss him on the lips so he knows
you aren't afraid,

but you will murder in their infancy the mewling
    memories
(how his moustache tasted
in your beard).

When the hell is he going to die anyway?
He's been sick for three fucking years!
His strength is gone, his lungs collapsed.
The doctors, you are told, have flushed his lungs
with tetracycline:
the searing bronchial flesh
scars closed the holes the infection bores.
Heal *that* pain, you positive thinkers.
Calm *that* horror in the night.

And still the clown in him
pratfalls
in letters Demerol dictates
in a sloppy hand.

Still he plops down on his
whoopee cushion of life and
cuddles in his lesioned arms
those whose fear of death is
greater than his own.

You will *not* respect him.
You will *not* pray.
You will think how fine
you're getting along without him already.
After all
he's only a man you carelessly let in on your truth
before you knew he'd tear it from you and drag it
into a grave.

Over and over
the conversation of others
measures weeks,
then days.
As the remaining reports
grow grim,
someone is whispering words like
release,
plane of consciousness,
crossing over, and *letting go.*

Think how much better it will be for him
and for you

and his vigilant sisters
whose children stare puzzled into
      babysitters' eyes
and for his shellshocked mother
golfing his hospital time away,
the greens as smooth as tombstones.

Denial is a tricky business.

When the call comes—
early on Sunday morning,
as all the calls seem to come these days,
over bagels and coffee
and the ruins of your life—
the soothing voice of Sharon
midwifes the news.

And you knew it would come
and you knew it would come soon
but still your heart will clench like a sea creature
under attack,
will turn on itself and spew venom.
And the only words that mean at all are
Clark and
dead.

Your preparations have been
in vain; willy-nilly the

weeping begins, though he was nothing at all
but your next of skin,
and the weeping does not stop
all day
and your mind will hear nothing
all day
but a question:

When
at last
will this *God* of theirs
grow bored
with tears?

Postcard from Paris

"Dear Clark,
I finally made it to France.
You were ten days dead.
Paris was weeping."

The cherubim on the Pont Alexandre were weeping.
In the Louvre the Mona Lisa and the
Venus de Milo were weeping,
but the guard kept shouting *No Pictures!*

I dropped ten francs into a black tin box and
lit a candle for you in the Madeleine,
and Our Lady began weeping in the firelight.
The Virgin at Notre-Dame began weeping too
when I told her, and the ghost of Quasimodo
when his towering bells shook with the news.

In the Tuileries the boys and girls at boats were
      weeping
and the Africans peddling mechanical flying birds
and all the nude male statuary was weeping
and the waiters playing badminton under chestnut
      trees.
The hustlers by the Orangerie were weeping
and the gendarme by the Jeu de Paume.

In the Musée d'Orsay van Gogh was weeping blue
    pigment
and Manet was weeping at *dejeuner sur l'herbe*.
The nuns at the top of the Tour Eiffel were weeping
and the condescending tourists at the Deux Magots
and the Mediterranean leathermen of the Marais
and the predictable painters in Montmartre
and the homeless druggies of the Place St. Michel—
all of them weeping for loss of you.

I bought a postcard of a Greek youth
from a vendor near the Quartier Latin
and wrote on the back
in black ink:
"Dear Clark,
I finally made it to France.
You were ten days dead.
Paris was weeping."

Then I wrote your address in San Francisco
where your sisters would be sorting belongings for
    weeks
and I stood on a long line in a post office and
bought a stamp—air mail, special delivery.

Then I went to the bridge near the Sainte Chapelle
and tore it to pieces and sent it—air mail—
into the Seine.

And I thought, as I turned my back on water:
"Miss you.
Wish you
were here."

How to watch your brother die

For Carl Morse

When the call comes, be calm.
Say to your wife, "My brother is dying. I have to fly
to California."
Try not to be shocked that he already looks like
a cadaver.
Say to the young man sitting by your brother's side,
"I'm his brother."
Try not to be shocked when the young man says,
"I'm his lover. Thanks for coming."

Listen to the doctor with a steel face on.
Sign the necessary forms.
Tell the doctor you will take care of everything.
Wonder why doctors are so remote.

Watch the lover's eyes as they stare into
your brother's eyes as they stare into
space.
Wonder what they see there.
Remember the time he was jealous and
opened your eyebrow with a sharp stick.
Forgive him out loud
even if he can't
understand you.
Realize the scar will be
all that's left of him.

Over coffee in the hospital cafeteria
say to the lover, "You're an extremely good-looking
young man."
Hear him say,
"I never thought I was good enough looking to
deserve your brother."

Watch the tears well up in his eyes. Say,
"I'm sorry. I don't know what it means to be
the lover of another man."
Hear him say,
"It's just like a wife, only the commitment is
deeper because the odds against you are so much
greater."
Say nothing, but
take his hand like a brother's.

Drive to Mexico for unproven drugs that might
help him live longer.
Explain what they are to the border guard.
Fill with rage when he informs you,
"You can't bring those across."
Begin to grow loud.
Feel the lover's hand on your arm
restraining you. See in the guard's eye
how much a man can hate another man.
Say to the lover, "How can you stand it?"
Hear him say, "You get used to it."
Think of one of your children getting used to
another man's hatred.

Call your wife on the telephone. Tell her,
"He hasn't much time.
I'll be home soon." Before you hang up say,
"How could anyone's commitment be deeper than
a husband and wife?" Hear her say,
"Please. I don't want to know all the details."

When he slips into an irrevocable coma,
hold his lover in your arms while he sobs,
no longer strong. Wonder how much longer
you will be able to be strong.
Feel how it feels to hold a man in your arms
whose arms are used to holding men.
Offer God anything to bring your brother back.
Know you have nothing God could possibly want.
Curse God, but do not
abandon Him.

Stare at the face of the funeral director
when he tells you he will not
embalm the body for fear of
contamination. Let him see in your eyes
how much a man can hate another man.

Stand beside a casket covered in flowers,
white flowers. Say,
"Thank you for coming," to each of several hundred
     men
who file past in tears, some of them
holding hands. Know that your brother's life
was not what you imagined. Overhear two

mourners say, "I wonder who'll be next?" and
"I don't care anymore,
as long as it isn't you."

Arrange to take an early flight home.
His lover will drive you to the airport.
When your flight is announced say,
awkwardly, "If I can do anything, please
let me know." Do not flinch when he says,
"Forgive yourself for not wanting to know him
after he told you. He did."
Stop and let it soak in. Say,
"He forgave me, or he knew himself?"
"Both," the lover will say, not knowing what else
to do. Hold him like a brother while he
kisses you on the cheek. Think that
you haven't been kissed by a man since
your father died. Think,
"This is no moment not to be strong."

Fly first class and drink Scotch. Stroke
your split eyebrow with a finger and
think of your brother alive. Smile
at the memory and think
how your children will feel in your arms,
warm and friendly and without challenge.

AIDS haiku

Laughter in the garden
echoes through time.
Jasmine moon.

A letter from Kenny.
One sentence. The news.
The news. Fear.

Jacaranda blooms purple;
the bruise of an eye.
Spring. An ending.

—

Summer nights on
Twin Peaks, the disease
incurable as fog.

Blistering sun.
Blistered skin.
Life blisters.

—

Dropping like flies,
young friends are
rhyme without meter.

Purple flowers.
Purple lesions.
Heart. Heart. Lungs.

—

A winter moon.
A muffled cry.
A long slow death.

Gasping for breath.
Asking for water.
Grasping at straws.

Wasted to nothing, smiling:
in the sisterly light,
peace comes to the silver fox.

Frost on the pine cones.
Lake Tahoe dawn.
Kenny dying.

When Kenny died

How does the poem know
that Kenny has died?
How does it know the way of the ink
that runs from the pen as smooth as
life from the lungs of a friend
who held Venus in his hand
and juggled the rings of Saturn
to prove there was life on Earth
at least before his leaving it?

How does the perfume know
that smelled so different once
on his skin and my own?
How does it know to change on me
to smell of him
now that Kenny has died?

And how do the pine trees know
to stand unmoving
in the evening breeze?
And how does my mother know
who calls to comfort
because she caught a chill
tying on her apron to
cook an evening meal?

And how does sorrow know
who whispers his name
in my inner ear?

Kenny is dead, it says.
Is dead.
Is dead.

And I am waiting still
for Kenny to come
and take my hand
and cushion the pain
with the pillow
of his smile.

How to visit
the grave of a friend

For Kenneth Fermoyle

Wait until it's a hundred and five in the shade:
you will be
alone.
Wait until your car can barely make it
over the hill from Hollywood:
you will be
grateful
to be there.
Wear
white, the Japanese color of mourning. Marry
your sadness in the color white. Carry
your camera in case you need
a filter
to live through.

Approach slowly. Conserve emotion.
Feel the tears come to bask on your eyelids like
stray cats on the window sills of Greek widows.
Feel the hair on your arms begin to rustle
like wheat in wind. Birds will rustle
in the underbrush. Your throat will flutter
like a nightingale, but no song will come.

Read the marker, flat in the grass.
Remember you had forgotten his middle name.
Subtract
the year of his birth from the year of his
death. Say "twenty-six" out loud as if
this could not possibly be
the difference.

Read the inscription again. It is his own
words: "In light of what you see,
What shadows do I cast?"
Remember you have never before visited
the grave of a friend. Remember the day of his
funeral, the white balloons released
into a cool, high sky, empty as
his grandmother's eyes.

Remember the color of light in his hair,
how his ribs felt in your palm.
Forget what to do next. Return home
in the sweltering heat. Write
on a sheet of white paper:
"In light of what you see,
What shadows do I cast?"
Say the words aloud.
Feel the golden band on the
cormorant's neck.
Wonder if life will ever feel like something
other than death.

Gone

After the after
the beginning of
nothing appears.
Reminders linger:
your hair
in the bathroom
one by one;
all that glitters
a blue sequin from
last Halloween
stuck in the carpet
under the bed.
Time after time
I look up and
you are not there.
How much you are not there
is all my looking.
How deep you are not there
is how I burst into
kitchen tears to discover
the curry is empty
after all
these years.

Student teacher

For Carmine Barcia,
later known as Michael Carmine

Oh Carmine,
I fell for your thighs
hard and fast as a meteor
in the Eden of time,
you all eyes and incarnate skin,
brown and brown,
spun sugar of a port rich
in treasures, your ardor
outgrowing your ribs.

Younger by a league,
you were the magus of the caves
and high places. In
copious affection, you
held my hand and took me in
without forbidden planets ever
touching. I
could have lived
between your legs the
seven ages of man. Your No
was a doomsday hurdle I did not
soon get over.

The sharp news of your death
hooked my ear when I was most
unarmed: sodden with envy,
in lost pursuit of a charmer
named Dale—
a blond and blue-eyed you
who would decline with
just your grace and
kisses gentle as
unaspirated vowels.

Then flashing gold in the
bamboo roots, your name was
caught
among the dead, as it was
before you changed it half
to mine. It was Jim
who told me how you died: home,
wrapped in your mother's
tongue, cradled again, tearing
her in the leaving of life
as you did in late
arrival.

I should have wept, but
hid my head inside the
leather and manwork scent of
Jim, muffling a guttural howl.

I wept the bayou dry
in the salad days
of plague.

So I am hoarse again
and left behind to
mourn with words the
fleeting reggae laughter
of a memory dressed to play in
appetite. Had you fallen
into the orbit of my lust
and given in to the plain love
I offered,
perhaps we'd both have died,
or you would not,
and I might not have dropped
whatever reason I thought I had
to live
into the hurt silence between
unmade sounds. Survival
is an empty business, noble as
usury, remote
as a star.

And I think our God must be
a selfish and a
teasing bitch to
dangle dancing Carmines

before adoring eyes and
yank them back to
hoard. I heard Him
in the Santa Ana winds,
roaring in His garden full of
crimson you, smooth to His beard
as the imagined loving
of a wise youth once was
to a livelier,
uncautious me.

Real-life dreams

"Old friends are the great blessing of one's later years."—Horace Walpole (1717-1797)

It was winter
and I dreamed my left hand was full of ice.
When I woke up I found it was just that my hand
had come out of the covers, and it was cold.

I woke up and went into the bathroom and
looked into the mirror with one eye,
the other still clogged with sleep,
and I didn't know the face I saw there.
It was bearded, freckled, red-haired and
handsome. Even the bathroom had been
transformed. Someone had circled the vanity
in flowers. The stranger in the mirror was
thin; there were bone bumps on his shoulders
and his wicker chest was a hairless boy's,
not a graying bearish man's.
I must have slept for months, I thought,
and I've wakened now, and I'm wasting away
with the plague, but I didn't feel ill.

Then my laughing Clark came into the bathroom
cracking jokes, and the flowers suddenly made
as much sense as mismatched high-topped sneakers.

I realized who I was and that I was
healthy, and that I had slept for some months
and wakened to life just the way I would have
    sketched it,
if I could draw anything but erroneous conclusions.
In the dining room, I ran into kind, sagacious Kenny.
Do you live here too? I asked, and he didn't
answer, but his paintings hung
in the apartment, which was paneled in dark wood
and enormous, with rooms I had forgotten,
and that Kenny and Clark hadn't even found
while waiting for me to wake into
what I always knew I was. And the three of us
laughed as we always did, and I couldn't believe my
luck: I lived with my two best friends in a wonderful
home, and I was beautiful and happy, and I was so
filled with life, I was overcome with
joy and gratitude and the
divine order of all things.

It was only that my left hand was full of ice.
When I woke up I found it was just that my hand
had come out of the covers, and it was cold.
I was still old and fat,
my apartment was still a damp and drafty dump,
Kenny and Clark were still dead,
and I was so filled with life
I was weeping before my first cup of tea.

Later I tried to thank some god or other for
letting me feel asleep what I'd never know awake,
but there wasn't much conviction in it.
And I couldn't get my left hand warm
no matter what I did,
even when I plunged it between my legs
to scratch the skin off a
new and painful rash.

Old friends are the great blessing of one's
later years. And so are fingernails.

V.
Barricades and Trenches

Hair again

She wants to know
why I'm growing it again,
after the hair wars of the '60s.
"I'll be able to braid it soon,"
were her first words after
six months apart,
her overclose embrace
demanding an honest response.

But how do you look your mother in the eye
when she comes back clipped and pruned
from the mini-mall beauty parlor
and tell her
you have become Rapunzel
in a tower of despair,
that your hair
is the golden fleece
the quilters need
to stitch the names
of the dead?

"It's too short to braid,"
I reply, pulling away,
"though it looks okay
in pigtails."

See, she just can't picture
Veronica Lake at a suit and tie
business lunch. But Mom, doll,
I only wear ties to
dine with you in places that
require discomfort.
I admit I was wrong, getting tar
on the velvet Fauntleroy suit back in '52,
but long hair looks fine with
whatever I wear,
including my tux for those
fabulous fund-raisers
I'm going to all the time
between funerals.

Yeah, it's long
and feels like it should have
twenty years ago, before I knew what
sensual was, before dark Julius
filled his opera vowels
and lower register
with awakening me.
I like the cobweb curl of it,
the shudder that
takes me by storm when a
vagabond strand
licks my neck
like the tongues of

strangers once did,
when an ass in the dark wasn't
filled with death juice.

I could tell her that
during the commercials.

I could tell her
this is the hair that Kenny kissed
before he died,
that Clark fondled the last time
I saw him alive.
Or that the light in my hair
holds the laughter of
Dennis Akazawa like music
in amber—that
giggling gentle man who
wrapped my desire
in his desire
and turned our bodies to
bodies each time we
touched. If I cut it,
I would lose some part of them.

I remember, *madre*:
you brushed it with silver
when it went platinum from
toddling in the sun;

slashed it with hazel scimitars
when I was an auburn walrus.
It was bountiful then
and yours by bondslave right.
Now it's graying and
stiff around the ears with
survivor shame, but the thinning crop
is all my own, my bald patch posted to
put poachers on notice:
Private Property—Keep Out.

No, no red-haired Delilah will
slice off my life with a
mind so narrow a son could
slit his wrists on it.

It's only hair,
my last chance at youth;
boys like it sometimes, and touch it
kindly. It distracts me from
what life has become, and
keeps me from slaughtering the
firstborn of the gentiles
each night before I sleep
on pillows of my hair.

My dreams are lost
in a witch's forest;

my hair trails in the wind,
a whited comet's tail
tangled in the heart branches.
I shout your name, but
the huntsmen all are dead.
And the wolves—
the howling wolves—
are hungry
for blood.

Piss Jesse, or
Silence = Death

For Tim Miller,
artist, activist, hero

"I am accustomed to speak my
opinion unreservedly; this has
occasioned me some misfortune,
but I do not therefore cease to speak
as I think. Language is given us to
express ideas—he who fetters it is
a bigot and a tyrant."
— Percy Bysshe Shelley

Uh-oh,
pee-pees are a
no-no!
The Senior Senator from
North Carolina told me so.
Jesse Helms is going down on history—
in history, I mean, of course—as a
dingaling dickhead from the tired Old South
and Congress has no balls,
so Art's not allowed to have any
either. Ain't that right,
Corcoran Gallery?

Uh-oh say can you see
why the legislature loves war so much?
'Cause it blows the family jewels off
so many brave men and true,
leaving Midwestern vaginas empty
for the poking, probing fingers
of the Bible Belt's elected elite.
Jesse loves the smell of cunt juice
on his conscience.

Don't touch that dial!
We'll be right back with more
doo-doos and don'ts from
Capitalist Hill.
Your ass is in a sling, boy,
and it's going to the highest bidder,
so bend over and say
Ahhhhhh'm a Yankee Doodle
and that feels just *dandy!*

Dear Santa,
What I want for Christmas is
a stake through the heart of
the Senior Senator from North Carolina,
preferably a stake
smeared with the scared shit
of the House of Reprehensibles.

Uh-oh beautiful facetious skies...
America is a dung hill; our
politicians are maggots.
So squashing Jesse Helms like a boll weevil
wouldn't be like real killing
at all. Real killing would be what
tobacco does.

Uh-oh,
the FBI says
threats are a
no-no!—and they should know,
they've made enough of 'em—
so nobody should off
Jesse Helms.
It would be wrong.
It would be fun to watch, though.
We could all march out
to the National Cemetery
and write obscene graffiti on his
tombstone with the blood of
Central Americans Jesse has decided
must go, must go, and spend the afternoon
fuckity-fuck-fuck-fucking on his
chilly, chilly grave,
using the flag to wipe cum
off our Old Glory holes
(since that's all the Stars 'n' Bars is

good for anymore—Don't ask me to stand up
for the *Scar Mangled Banner*).

Jealous Jesse has a wicked case of
pussy passion, and a pecker the size
of a hummingbird's bill, and
what pisses him off sincerely is that
his wife won't fist him up to her elbow,
'cause she's got Christ with a boner
tattooed on her forearm, and she don't
want Him covered with rectal muck
(Jesse douches, to be sure, and empties his
enema bag directly into the platform
of the Reptilian Party).

Columbia the scum of the ocean...

Uh-oh,
I haven't
offended anyone,
have I?
I haven't made anyone *uncomfortable?*
That *would* be a caterwauling shame.
An offensive poem could
bring down the U.S. Constitution
faster than a racist Republican—
not naming any names, mind you, so
take your pick (it's easy).

Pollution starts in the Senate,
proliferates in the inaction of the
House, prospers in
tax incentives for the rich
proposed by the White House on
fishing trips dressed by
L.L. Bean—don't let the
big one get away unscathed.

Uh-oh,
I'm stepping on toes,
but that's a
no-no!—my tango teacher
told me so.
Art's s'posed'ta be
polite. That's only
right. Very *far*
right. Do not go gentle
into that. *Fight!*

A modest proposal, overtly political

For Jim Pickett and ACT UP/L.A.

I have a dream.
Well, there's nothing unique in that:
we all have dreams—
or so the psychiatricks tell us,
but then those are the same KKKlowns
who wrote us all off as weirdosickoperverts
all those long years, so
maybe they don't know their
asses from a Freudian phallus.

My dream is this:
I gobble down all the plastic explosives
all the terrorists ever got hold of,
then dress up in a tuxedo—
Calvin Klein, Bill Blass perhaps, something classic,
understated—
then I sashay into a White House ball
and detonate myself on foie gras and Brie.

Now, I'd be dead, of course,
which is one of the snags I haven't worked out,
but so would they—
all the politicians in the country
in one historic bang:

all the lying schemers
who make laws against us over three-martini lunches
at taxpayers' expense and who
flip the bird at conscience to win their districts,
who novocaine their ethics to impress their drooly-
    tongued constituents and
wrap their flaccid lips around the rhetoric of hate;

and all those crypto-fascist Christ-money mongers,
including that dickless Polack pope in his white
    sheet—

don't tell me not to buy into their hatred!
I've been hating them since before they knew
who or what I am
(my anger is the legacy of their cruelty,
my rage is the birthright of the outcast)—

and all the ex-presidents in mansions in Bel-Air
so layered in latex you couldn't detect a facial twitch
if you rammed his oft-probed ass with a flagpole;

and all the chiefs of police with itchy trigger fingers,
choke holds, and Republican aspirations;

all of them up in smoke in the twinkling of an eye.

All right.
I know.

It's a futile
fantasy,
but I have another, and it goes like this:

Once,
just once,
all the heterosexuals get together and do one decent
     thing
just because it's right.

You can stop laughing now.

Try this one:

Every time one of us dies of the plague,
we give a gun and ten bullets to the lovers
who are forbidden obituary mentions in the
L.A. or New York *Times*, the *Washington Post*
and *Boston Globe* and *Miami Herald* and *Chicago
Tribune*—all the homophobic rags run by
impotent intelleggshells who think being Jewish is
an excuse for having no compassion—
and we give the lovers a list of the "innocent"
(chosen at random),
people who haven't done a thing to "deserve dying."

And all the lovers who do not exist would take a bullet
and blast it up the ass of one of these "victims"—
the way Franco's firing squad executed our Lorca

for his Latin love—
and when ten of them die for every one of us
(just to keep the death rate even-Steven)
then, and maybe only then,
will some white heterosexual Midwestern male
sit up in the middle of a Christian night and say,
"Enough. It has to stop!"
And it would.

The cure would be found by the end of the week,
and it would only cost us
2.7 stealth bombers and a dozen nuclear missiles,
and the robber barons of the pharmaceutical
        companies,
caught off guard by grief, would let their greed down
for a minute and give away the medication that
        would make
all the infections evaporate like
campaign promises after elections.
And God (more reclusive than Marlon Brando even)
would make a rare exception and
grant a single interview to the alternative press
to say that he's PISSED OFF that people are
DUMPING SHIT on his GAY CHILDREN. Then he'd
raise all the AIDS dead from their graves and
unscatter their ashes, and
all the lovers who do not exist would be loving again,
and loving would be everywhere and everyday,
all the tears would be unshed,

all the flowers of the funeral wreaths
would be unpicked and would
cover the earth with blossoms.
And the hate-hoarding heterosexuals who
beat us and
cut us and
strung us up and
burned us down and
ripped off our brain cells and
poured hot mercury into our open veins,
and who taught us to do all these things to ourselves,
would see the joy of a hundred thousand men
reunited with a hundred thousand men and their
twenty million friends.

And all the heterosexuals on earth and in hell would
get down on their knees—
their religions as powerless to help them
as they were to help us—
and they would implore us for absolution,
would say they were sorry on network television
every hour for nine hundred years,
and then,
maybe then,
we would think about forgiveness,
if we weren't too busy with our own lives
to care.

Statues of liberty

Michael Woo,
the only Asian-American member of the
Los Angeles City Council, makes a motion and
flags are lowered to half staff for
the dead of Tian An Men Square, and why not?

The slaughter of innocents must have symbols.

But where are the half-mast
star-spangled banners for the
AIDS dead—
the lovers, brothers, sons,
children strapped to wheelchairs,
their futures bound tightly in hospital tubes
and hung from the rearview mirror of history?

The dead of Beijing are many.
The AIDS dead are many times many.

The President,
between jogging and jockeying for power,
praises the valor of one fearless man
prepared to give his life
to stop a stink of tanks bearing down
on the city, and why not?

The home of the brave needs inspiration.

But what of the courage
of every woman and man who meets death
with lesions on the brain,
the fortitude of those who know they will die
but go on living anyway,
tens or hundreds of thousands
for whom democracy and its goddesses
are as relevant as
lead crystal and bone china,
who are mowed down by neglect and
self-serving ignorance,
as potent and profitable here as there?

Where are the headlines of heroism
for the AIDS dead, my intrepid friends?

Do not misunderstand,
I am not callous, unfeeling, parochial:

On the fourteenth of May, I stood beside
the students of Tian An Men Square.
That Mother's Day,
this heart beat with their blood
and felt the hope in their hope-starved eyes.

I too wept as the news reports grew
bleaker and bloodier on the fourth of June.
There!
There, where that tank is rolling over a

string quartet, is the spot I stood to
shoot the portrait of Chairman Mao,
beaming from the Gate of Heavenly Peace.

I count them all among my own dead,
who died twice—in the crushed flesh of
a midnight's massacre, and the
smiling doublespeak of the propaganda dragon.

What has become of gentle Li of the Kunlun Hotel?
and knowing Wang of the Yangtze and Nanjing?
and handsome Chen Bao Xing of the Grand Canal?
men whose hands touched these hands,
whose fates are tangled now with the
prayers of an agnostic poet
trying to believe in God despite the evidence.

The martyrs of Tian An Men Square are
more noble than their principles;
they are the fallen heroes the monument signifies;
they are properly entombed in our rage.

But who in the world mourns the AIDS dead,
who did not die *for* democracy,
but *because* of it?

And who is building our statues?
Who bears our eternal torch
of truth?

The future cowards built

When there is no one left in the city but soldiers
our *oohs* and *ahs* will matter as little as frogs.
The headstones of those who were buried
will be covered by weeds and wildflowers.
The dogs that ate the corpses will have been
eaten by scavengers before the evacuation.
Our tears will have dried up
like the reservoirs, and
rain will be spoken of in hushed tones,
like art and childhood and melons.
No one will speak of the homosexuals—
not their parents, relocated to the country
like old blankets,
nor their children, in combat training abroad.
But it will not matter,
not to the infantrymen standing guard over ruins,
not to the generals laying siege to the ruins,
not to the statues in deserted streets swept clean
by nightwinds. After all, in a war
there are bound to be
casualties. The death toll began to mount
the moment war was declared,
when Uncle Sam, an out-of-work actor,
met the first diagnosis by declaring inconsequence.
It will end when students are afraid to murmur
justice

over cappuccino and clove cigarettes in a
leftist café, when
radical
is only an exponential number to catalogue the
disappeared. Our poems, of course,
will be forgotten, our books
burned with the others, our loves
scrubbed from paving stones with
undiluted lies.
All our cries aside, it will not
matter: it will be
over. And the over will
feed on itself until the hollowed O is
empty as a geode in a room too dark for
reflection.
And the darkness will spread like
hot tar on glass,
the sun will be drowned in the fear
of a coward's eye,
and this will be
their victory,
and our own.

VI.
Eros Reclaimed

Desire

He is hurrying home along a narrow street,
as he does each day at this time.
He is tall and dark, an Arab perhaps,
a prince of his own design.
Dust clings to his boots and jeans,
worn at the knees, torn.
He wears the same shirt every day,
a shirt that was green in a shop window.
It clings to his chest,
rides high above his middle, above
the muscles of his upper arms.
He carries a loaf of bread, a bottle of wine,
some meat and cheese.
He is hungry, yet remembers to look up to
your window and smile.
You are caught in his smile like an antelope
in the crosshairs of a hunter's rifle.
You sink into his smile.
You desire him. He is what
you desire.
You return his smile with a
wave, your mind invites him
to your room for supper.
Your inner ear hears his footsteps on the stair.
He smiles as he lays out the bread and wine,
meat and cheese; you lay out plates, a knife,

two glasses you stole from a café when no one
was looking. You eat in silence while he smiles,
his eyes crawl into your eyes for shelter.
You undress slowly never touching until you are
naked. In bed you
draw the smell of him inside your throat
(something that grows on trellises,
something of the underworld and wildlife).
The night is still. His skin is warm and dry,
his lips feed you. He is hard and male.
He is what
you desire,
if desire
must have an object.
He is hurrying home along a narrow street,
you wave but do not speak.
You hold the smell of him in your throat and
feel desire find your bloodstream.
Your room is lighted by
desire, your lover is
desire. It is wanting
that fills you, the moment before
the hour,
the waiting in your window for this smiling
stranger to appear,
to heat your legs,
to move your mind to stories
without endings,
to be your blood.

Daddy

Oh Daddy,
I'm far away and miss you
so much. The bogeyman is on the
prowl again, draped in last year's
judgment. Things go bump
in the cold sweaty night,
growl in the swelling neck and
sunken groin where men have danced
on points of pins
and Sabu rode his elephant
all the morning long in rain.

Kiss me quiet in the
moonless room. Tell me about
Heaven and good boys turn
to angels when they die;
how you'll be there to greet me—
like that dream of disembarking
in the Land of Dead and
Grandpa's Airedale Mickey
lumbered up to lick my hand—
how you played hooky from school and
snuck off to Broadway to
steal a piece of Fanny Brice;
and how God loved his only son
so much He killed him.

Remember the time we went to
Radio City and saw
Ben Hur from the first and only
row? You ate popcorn and were
Charlton Heston with
your arm around my chair,
your shoulder straining on the
reins. I was happy as Haya
Harareet to ride your chariot
anywhere.

I dreamed I was crucified once
but felt nothing, was shot as
many times as St. Sebastian
but did not complain, was
hoisted by a hook around my
breastbone—eyes skyward like
a saint or martyr—but
it did not hurt. That's how
pain is in dreams: all concave
terror, but pain in life is
terror and agony too. No wonder
passion can have two meanings.

And God whispered:
This is my beloved son in whom I am well pleased.
And Jesus was so moved

he gladly gave his life
for a stranger.

Oh Daddy,
all I ever wanted was to
crawl into your arms, as firm
as hairless Samson's buttock cheeks.
Naked and enslaved, he grunts the
prison treadmill round, trapezius muscles
rising to the task. You bought me that
beefcake Bible for my confirmation
and it more or less confirmed
what you feared.
I was grateful for
Samson's he-man flesh, for
Jesus' long untangled hair
and angels gentle as
bathing or Hedy Lamarr.

Oh Daddy,
wherever you are, I still want to
suck your chest hair, sink
into your skin like the
painless dream lashings of
a leather scourge, spread
tattoos across your stung trunk
like oil from Hedy's cruet
rubbed into the sore and

musk Semitic meat of Victor Mature
as John the Baptist—no!
that's not right (that was Rita
Hayworth dropping veils)—
as *Samson,* rather, pulling down
the temple by its columns,
loincloth stiff on glistening limbs
anointed by angry desire.

Secrets spill in the dark aisles
of theaters and churches
like blood from test tubes spreading
contagion. All I wanted was to
touch your cock that time
in the shower once when
I was small. Shame feels like
déjà vu these days, but still
I love a shower room full of
nude men dripping water through
marble swirls of hair.

Oh Daddy,
it was you all the time in those
backroom bars and bathhouse crannies
at four a.m.,
all those men who
filled me with the
Holy Spirit. I was

speaking in tongues. And when the
profane angel death comes
flapping down with winks and
wings akimbo, I will
recognize his sultry and
engendering breath, will
look into his bedroom eyes,
and see you there:
the dusky idol of my
'50s matinee,
strong and silent,
sullen as Gregory Peck's
lower lip lusting after
Bathsheba in a Technicolor dream.

In the port of the palms

You remember it as something thrilling, something exotic that could not have happened to you, a dream of some faraway place, the Canary Islands at dawn, yes, that might have been it, a September sunrise in Las Palmas, a Tuesday. And the warm darkness is shaken from the palm trees by the breakfast waiters, who joke with the cabbies left over from last night, from the last wave of guests to return from the disco downtown, the sound of leather soles on the gravel of the historic hotel, dark men in white short-sleeved shirts. And you are at the breakwater boulders, your eyes fixed on three young fishermen, brothers perhaps, pulling nothing from the sea in hand-held nets. The water is all the colors of blue near purple, the sky all the yellows there are. And the fish are not coming from the sea hand-over-hand into the small rowboat, but the young men work their sleek hard limbs and do not give up hoping. In the distance a score of tankers from the Middle East, freighters from India, are silhouetted at anchor. You bring your camera to your face. You hold your breath and click and click again to frame the memory. And then there is a man watching you as you are watching, with a sharp and practiced eye. He speaks in Spanish. You reply in this language you do not understand, but he has English ready, in reserve. He has a mustache and wears a jumpsuit of olive-green velour with red piping at the seams. He breaks thin ice with a comment about the pope and homosexuals. You are caught off guard, but you know now his mission. You stroll to the end of the breakwater and back, wishing him silently away, you circle the small marina of brightly colored boats in need of serious repair. There are Africans here, Asians, boats that have sailed more than a single sea, that have carried cargo proscribed by international agreement. He is married and has a lover named Ysidro who works as a guide for the tourist bureau. He is unhappy, he tells you haltingly, flirting, bumping his arm against yours as you walk. He tells you that he is becoming "strong." You do not catch the word. He repeats it, making a fist to illustrate his point. He asks if you are becoming "strong." You reply that, yes, you are becoming strong, meaning that you are growing inured to the blows life has been dealing lately. But he has mistranslated. He is meaning "hard." And he is indeed hard, under his olive velour, just thinking of your flesh on his flesh, as you stand now under the greening bronze fountain of naked adolescents in the flowering garden of the Hotel Santa Catalina. You remember it as a dream, the desire of an appliance merchant in the Canary Islands at dawn, a Tuesday in September, perhaps, his lust turned to you in the rising sun like no man's lust for longer than you can remember. You are frightened. You are flattered. You decline his offer, as kindly as you can. You are appalled by the undisguised need in his eyes, your eyes are riveted to the muscles of the sculpted boys who frolic now just above your heads. You are entranced by his greed, the color of your skin as you begin to bronze, the racing of your heart, the shortness of your breath, your gracious getaway, the gardeners raking litter from the gravel paths. It could only be a dream, to have been desired by accident like that, to have had a prayer answered like that, with no provocation at all.

Pioneering Cubism

*"It's not a reality you can take in
your hand. It's more like a perfume
... The scent is everywhere but you
don't quite know where it comes
from."* —Picasso on Cubism

*"We must go back to the human,
not to the man."* — Georges Braque

"Don't be shy."
—Vladimir, Brazilian porn star

The humidity was 99 percent; when it reached a
hundred, Hurricane Hugo would touch down on
Manhattan. MoMA smelled of wool recently
uncloseted from camphor; raindrops dappled the
mottled marble of the sculpture garden;
in the cafeteria a woman chewing on dentures
shuffled postcards over creamed spinach.

"You know what I'm saying?" someone said.

I held my hands across my face and inhaled
between my fingers. They smelled of a Cubist
brochure, but Vladimir lingered.

Before Pablo was "Picasso" or Georges "Braque,"

they were painters, pigment brothers bent on
revolution, Orville and Wilbur Wright in the vortex
of Hurricane Gertrude's Parisart, their brushes
kissing the same palette like two men licking the
same erection, climaxing together, if you please,
in the Pyrenees, summer of 1911.

I came behind the screen at the Gaiety Burlesk
wrapped in Vladimir's amazing arms, bulging
burl wood of the Amazon. Half Brazilian Portugese,
half rain forest Indian, he's named for the vampire
in a Dracula movie his mother was fond of.
Since I saw him first, on videotape, he has haunted
my dreams, a hunter in war colors
crouching in the bush, his darting eye ironic
as Gotham, hairless skin smooth as river pebbles.

He caught my adulating glance and knew I had
cash.

"Almost every evening," Picasso wrote, "either I
went to Braque's studio or he came to mine. Each of
us *had* to see what the other had done during the
day." Just as I had to flee the posh hotel to bask in
whatever wonder Vladimir had accomplished at the
gym; how much higher would his mounded chest
rise in the flood tide of my admiration?

Fact is, they were not well-matched, the feisty
Spaniard quick as a hummingbird in search of
nectar, sniffing after skirt and fame, the Frenchman
slower in hand than brain, slower still when he
caught a war wound (shrapnel fever).
Vladimir was the sound of one hand clapping the
bare canvas of my hairy ass.

*[Rushing noise of a man breathing sharply through
his nose, then a long and tenor nasal sigh, like air
through narrow bamboo.]*

The 'teens brought Pablo and Georges to the
turning point; two twenties bought me Vladimir. I
didn't know where to land the opening brushstroke.
He kissed with closed lips, then wrapped his mouth
around my rough neck. Nearby the other dancers
loitered, *les demoiselles d'Avignon*, fierce, primal,
scented with earthy lotions and preening in the
strobe-heated glare of strangers who knew their
bodies as scalding triangles: isosceles lust.

I wore the odor of Vladimir's sultry groin like tight
leather gloves. It lasted when soap dried. I
carried the smell of his sweat in my beard.

Nicotine stained Picasso's fingers; Braque's hair
reeked of linseed. In the swirling cigar smoke, the

secret of intimates wafted from canvas to canvas
nipple.

He tasted sweet, like skin and mangoes.

A day later the storm had passed the city by,
pastrami with mustard had washed off the Vladimir
soap could not, but I refused to trim my nostril hair,
where he was embedded, lounging like an
odalisque flexed for business; and I kept wondering
if what two painters had in common was more a
predilection for each other than for gray and ochre.

If human odors were indelible, there would be less
hypocrisy. That's why Picasso and Braque used
permanent glue made from the corpses of animals:
to hold their fragments fast as figments.

There is paint and semen in the revolution of an hour.

And I am heading out into the night again
to put my mouth again on a Brazilian sex star
named Vladimir, whose man-aroma makes my
fingers itch, and whose libations give my hands the
strength of truth or fists or flowers, whose
asshole holds an essence fundamental as
paint on canvas, a line between two points direct as
flesh fused to flesh by capital desire.

Lord Byron takes leave of love

*"[At Missolonghi] Byron felt the last
latent stirrings of homosexual desire
and experienced his final passion in
an unconsummated love for a Greek
page, Loukas Chalandritsanos."*
— Louis Untermeyer
Lives of the Poets

I am dying slowly, Loukas,
in the cold outside your sun.
If Greece is warmth,
you are a jealous, warring Turk
eclipsing the heat I crave,
your dark eyes shadowed in doubt.
Your new jacket fits snugly across
your back; your trousers too are
tight as fists. Your neck is carved
confusion.
Do not fear—I have grown weary of
weeping, and you will soon be free:
death lies here between us
in the icy Missolonghi rain,
in the vision of my mother,
heartless at times as the leather
of your arm, chill as
desire worn out by

satisfaction.
My regrets weigh on me
like blankets that offer
neither comfort nor protection:
I squandered passion,
spilled my lust in unadoring beds;
women I spurned when
pleasures thinned
ran mad with their *amours*
as now, even near death,
I long to fold into your
hot young breast, the inky hair as coarse
as hay. You are a horse
to ride into the Hellespont, a horse
to ride me to my sister's
shamed embrace.
I kiss the air where
I dreamed you stood sentinel,
offer my lips to the damp night,
my wild and absent boy.
I dreamed you played my body
skillfully in summer sin and
lit the core of me; I raced with you
on two good legs. I write for you, but
generations yet to come—
envious as a child—
will keep you guarded, out of sight.
They brand you Caliban

and bind you to the rock of
ignorance.
That is our fate, to be
reviled, to be reviling.
You could have stayed until the end.
It won't be long—
the breath of a daughter lost,
the rhyme of a storm-drowned friend.
You are gone but
held forever in the fire
some future men will light in our
memory, never knowing our names.
They will have no doubts,
will hold each other close in life
and whisper into dying ears
the names their love has known.
My sweet olive of the Peloponnese,
you are the last and best of me;
I have become myself in praising you,
the omega of my alphabet,
my peacock,
my pillow,
my sleep.

Sammy

Sammy's dancing last
down to his skivvies.
He's a dark and
hirsute Greek who
carries in his smile
all you feel when you
see the Acropolis.
He likes you, Sammy
does, which is not
surprising given
how many dollars you've
tucked into his G-string.

He's yours forever
when he's dancing.
After he's as
gone as a lover who's
already left you but
hasn't left home.

Evoë Sammy! Dance!

His moistening hair
drips sweat that snakes
around his neck; his
toddler's grin is

lost in itself like
your reason to live.

Oh Sammy,
bacchant boy,
you are the thing
that died in me
when all my brothers died,
when Ben looked
last across our
long love and said,
"I'm sorry," and
I knew he was
packing on the sly.
My mouth is ripe
for your dangerous
fluids, my cock is
hard and aimed in
your direction.

And now he twirls,
now bends,
now offers himself
like a severed head
on a silver charger:
his smile askew,
your face
between his legs.

The music pounds
in your eyes.
You see shore.
You kiss him wet
with singles.

VII.
How to Choose Life

How to choose life

For those who come after

Put off the decision for as long as you can.
Wait until your body has begun
to decline,
until you are swollen with food swallowed
to keep from gagging on hunger.

Many will have died. You will have made
lists, wept at funerals, made excuses.
You will not be one of the nurturing ones,
not yet.
You will be He Who Mourns.

One will hurt the most.
For three days
you will weep whenever your mind
reads his name aloud like a mother
calling her child to dinner.
For three days you will weep, and your red eyes
will suddenly realize that the weeping has not
begun. It will come in waves like
calendar pages, like autumns dropping
needles into stacks of leaves as
dry and brittle as the skin of
one whose body sang once with life

on mountaintops with eagles in the snow,
in deserts and in cool dim rooms.

Wait.
Wait.
Do not rush. As rash a decision
as you now might make must not be
hurried,
cannot be made
before its time.

The time will be
the Day of All Saints.
You will be paying bills at your desk when
the Santa Ana winds blow open the casement windows
with Mojave howling.
It will be exactly noon on the Elgin
your mother gave your father on their wedding day
the year before Pearl Harbor.

There is nothing to do but laundry,
nothing to do but read the inscription
on your father's watch,
sink into the expression in your dead friend's eyes,
see a film about Nazis and Jews, and know
you have decided to live after all.

At midnight you will sit again at your desk.

You will remember younger days when
strangers approached just to touch
your tan, remember the first time you saw the man
you will see again only in photographs.
You will even remember
joy.

No lover will be returning home to your arms
this night. You will go alone
to a too warm bed
having chosen to dance
in the mouth of death
and will pray for the strength
to dance again
tomorrow.